EXPLORING SCIENCE

WAVES

ENERGY ON THE MOVE

BY DARLENE R. STILLE

Content Adviser: Paul Ohmann, Ph.D., Assistant Professor
of Physics, University of St. Thomas, St. Paul, Minnesota

Science Adviser: Terrence E. Young Jr., M.Ed., M.L.S.,
Jefferson Parish (Louisiana) Public School System

Reading Adviser: Susan Kesselring, M.A., Literacy Educator,
Rosemount-Apple Valley-Eagan (Minnesota) School District

Compass Point Books • 3109 West 50th Street, #115 • Minneapolis, MN 55410

Visit Compass Point Books on the Internet at www.compasspointbooks.com
or e-mail your request to custserv@compasspointbooks.com

Photographs ©: Steve Wilkings/Corbis, cover; Digital Vision, 4, 8–9, 26; Robert Holmgren/Peter Arnold, Inc., 5; OneBlueShoe, 6; Corbis, 7; Richard Hamilton Smith, 11; Fritz Polking/Peter Arnold, Inc., 12; Tom Vezo/Peter Arnold, Inc., 13; Scott Barbour/Getty Images, 15; Bruce Burkhardt/Corbis, 16; Brenda Matthiesen/Unicorn Stock Photos, 17; James H. Karales/Peter Arnold, Inc., 18; Jeffrey L. Rotman/Corbis, 21; Library of Congress, 28; Hulton Archive/Getty Images, 29, 43; David H. Wells/Corbis, 31; Henry Guttmann/Getty Images, 32 (top); Leonard Lessin/Peter Arnold, Inc., 32 (bottom); Joe McNally/Getty Images, 35; National Radio Astronomy Observatory/AUI/NSF, 36; Altitude/Peter Arnold, Inc., 37; Roger Ressmeyer/Corbis, 40; Yuri Cortez/AFP/Getty Images, 44; Tim Masterson/ Corbis, 46.

Editor: Nadia Higgins
Designer/Page Production: The Design Lab
Lead Designer: Jaime Martins
Photo Researcher: Marcie C. Spence
Cartographer: XNR Productions, Inc.
Illustrator: Farhana Hossain
Educational Consultant: Diane Smolinski

Managing Editor: Catherine Neitge
Creative Director: Keith Griffin
Editorial Director: Carol Jones

Library of Congress Cataloging-in-Publication Data
Stille, Darlene R.
Waves : energy on the move / by Darlene R. Stille.
p. cm. — (Exploring science)
Includes bibliographical references and index.
ISBN 0-7565-1259-X
1. Waves—Juvenile literature. 2. Wave-motion, Theory of—Juvenile literature.
I. Title. II. Exploring science (Minneapolis, Minn.)
QC157.S785 2006
531'.1133—dc22   2005002477

About the Author

Darlene R. Stille is a science writer and author of more than 70 books for young people. When she was in high school, she fell in love with science. While attending the University of Illinois, she discovered that she also loved writing. She was fortunate enough to find a career as an editor and writer that allowed her to combine both of her interests. Darlene Stille now lives and writes in Michigan.

TABLE OF CONTENTS

What Is a Wave?

A SURFER PADDLES out to sea, facedown on a surf-board. The surfer floats on the gently moving water and waits. Suddenly, here it comes! Water in the distance seems to pile up higher and higher. The surfer carefully stands up and balances on the board just in time to catch the big wave as it towers up and rushes toward the shore. White foam streaks across the top of the wave. The surfer glides down the front of the wave, riding in toward shallower water. With a tumble of white foam, the wave and surfer both disappear. The wave is gone, but the surfer bobs up and starts to paddle back out, ready to catch the next big one.

Expert surfers know a lot about how waves behave. They need to anticipate how a wave is going to break so they can catch the wave at the ideal moment.

MAKING WAVES

Surfers ride on water waves. But there are many other kinds of waves, such as sound waves and light waves. Visible light waves, radio waves, and X-rays are all called electromagnetic waves. "Surfers" on the Internet "ride" electromagnetic waves in search of all kinds of information. No matter what kind of waves you surf, all waves have one thing in common: Waves carry energy.

We can't see energy, but we can see what energy does. Waves are energy moving through something such as air or water. The "something" that waves move through is called the medium. Waves are a disturbance in the medium.

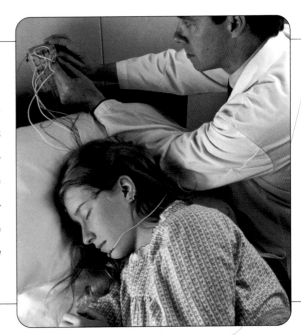

DID YOU KNOW?

BRAIN WAVES

The brain produces electrical waves that can be detected by special machines. Asleep or awake, the brain produces waves. In deep sleep, the waves grow slower and longer.

It is easy to see a wave move through a rope. Tie one end of the rope to a pole or tree. Then make a disturbance by shaking the other end up and down. A wave moves through the rope from one end to the other. The rope is the medium for the wave.

The wave moves forward through the rope, but the rope does not move forward. Only parts of the rope move up and down. This is important. Waves move forward through the medium, but unless the force that created the wave was exceptionally large, the medium itself does not move much. Waves move through water, but the water stays mostly in place. Sound waves move through air, but the air only vibrates a little bit.

A "human wave" is a good example of how waves travel without having the medium move very much. Doing the wave is a

As a wave moves through rope, the rope moves up and down, but it does not move forward.

popular activity at ball games. Someone gets the wave started by standing up and then sitting down. The next person stands up and sits down, and then the next person does the same thing. A human wave is like other waves in that the wave moves through the entire stadium, but the medium—each person—doesn't move very much. In a human wave, people don't move away from their seats. They just stand up and sit down.

Fans at a sporting event make a human wave by standing up one after the other. From a distance, it looks like a ripple is running through the crowd.

Shock Waves

A loud clap of thunder. The bang of a firecracker. The boom of a supersonic jet hurtling through the sound barrier. All these are examples of noises produced by shock waves.

Shock waves result from extreme pressure causing a disturbance in a medium such as air. A bolt of lightning superheats the

The Concorde was a supersonic jet that carried passengers from 1976 to 2003. It traveled at almost twice the speed of sound—and nearly three times as fast as regular commercial airplanes.

air around it, causing the air to expand rapidly. This rapidly expand-
ing air creates a shock wave. A jet traveling faster than the speed
of sound—1,116 feet (340 meters) per second at sea level—pushes
hard on the air in front of it, creating a shock wave. When the pressure of the shock wave reaches people's ears, they hear the crack
of thunder or the boom of a jet "breaking the sound barrier."

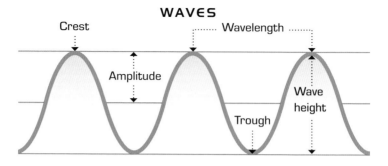

WAVES

Crest · · · · · · · · Wavelength · · · · · · · ·

Amplitude

Wave height

Trough

PARTS OF A WAVE

To understand what waves are and how they work, we need to know more about what a wave is like. First of all, waves are wavy. A simple wavy line on a piece of paper is a good representation of a wave.

As any surfer knows, every wave has a high point and a low point. The high point towers above the surfer. The surfer glides down toward the lowest point of the wave. The highest point of the wave is called its crest. The lowest point of the wave is called the trough.

How tall is a wave? The height of a wave is measured from its crest to its trough, or from top to bottom. Knowing wave height is important for boats and ships that go down into the trough of one wave and then must rise up to the crest of the next wave.

How long are the waves? Imagine a line from the top of one crest to the top of the next one, or from the bottom of one trough to another. The distance between the crests or troughs is one wavelength. Wavelength shows how close waves are to each other.

How do we measure a wave's strength? We find the amplitude. Imagine a straight line drawn horizontally across the wavy line, midway between the crests and troughs. The amplitude of a wave is the distance from the crest to this midpoint line. The larger the amplitude, the more powerful the wave.

Water Waves

IT IS EASY to see waves in water. But what causes the waves? Like most waves, water waves begin with a disturbance in the medium. A rock tossed into a still pond can make waves. The rock splashing into the pond carries energy, and the energy makes waves that ripple across the surface.

The waves go out in circles from the spot where the rock entered the water. A series of waves, like circles inside circles, spreads out from the center of the disturbance.

DID YOU KNOW?

HOW WATER MOVES

Waves do not move ocean water from place to place. That job is done by currents and circulation patterns. Currents are like rivers of water in the ocean. Some currents are colder than the surrounding water and some are warmer. Cold water also circulates up from the deep ocean as warmer, saltier water circulates down.

Boats and ships slicing through water make bow waves. The waves go out from the bow, or front of the ship, in a V shape. The faster a boat or ship goes, the bigger the bow wave it makes.

HOW WIND MAKES WAVES

Most waves on the ocean and on lakes are caused by wind. The wind blows on the surface and makes a disturbance in the water. The waves move in the same direction that the wind is blowing.

Wind is moving air, a mixture of invisible gases. The molecules of gases in the air rub up against molecules of water. Energy goes from the moving air to the water and makes waves. One wave pushes against the surrounding water, making further waves. Then these waves push against nearby water, which, in turn, makes even more waves. Water waves are energy moving away from the original disturbance.

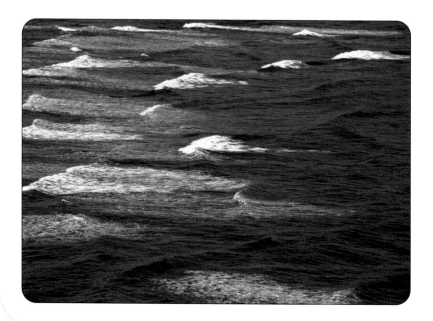

Winds blowing steadily across a wide ocean can make waves travel for thousands of miles.

The height of the waves depends on how strongly the wind is blowing and how long it has been blowing. A soft breeze makes small, gentle waves roll along the surface of the sea. Strong winds blowing for a long time cause bigger waves.

As waves move from deep water to shallow water, the waves slow down and start to change. The wavelengths grow shorter, and the crests grow taller. The taller crests indicate an increase in the waves' amplitude. Since amplitude is a measure of a wave's strength, the greater the amplitude, the more powerful the wave. When the wave grows tall enough, it breaks and releases its energy.

A wave breaks and releases its energy when its height is $\frac{1}{7}$ of its wavelength.

TSUNAMI, A KILLER WAVE

On December 26, 2004, the most powerful earthquake in 40 years was set off by a 600-mile-long (960-kilometer) break in Earth's crust. The break happened under the Indian Ocean, which is just off the coast of Indonesia, a country in Southeast Asia.

The movement of the earth displaced a huge amount of ocean water, triggering a series of tsunamis, which are gigantic waves. The word *tsunami* (pronounced sue-NAHM-ee) comes from two Japanese words meaning "harbor" and "wave." The waves went out from the site of the earthquake and traveled almost unnoticed toward the coasts of India, Indonesia, Thailand, and Sri Lanka. The tropical beaches were packed with unsuspecting tourists enjoying a holiday break.

In the open sea, ships are not likely to even notice a passing tsunami. That's because the wavelength of a tsunami in deep water can be as long as 300 miles (480 km), and its amplitude is very small, only a few feet.

A tsunami races through open ocean water at speeds of up to more than 500 miles (800 km) per hour. The wave slows down as it enters shallower water near the shore. As its speed slows, its amplitude increases greatly. These giant waves can rise up as high as 100 feet (30 m).

People along the Indian Ocean coasts on December 26, 2004, looked up to see a wall of water coming toward them. For many,

there was no time to escape. The tsunami crashed ashore, sweep-
ing away hotels and homes, buses and businesses, and even a railroad train. In Sri Lanka, the wave rushed more than one-half mile
(1 km) inland.

In an instant, the tsunami destroyed entire towns. Afterward,
rescue workers found more than 200,000 people dead and many
thousands more injured and homeless.

A girl in a coastal town in Sri Lanka looks at the remains
of a house after the devastating tsunami of 2004.

CHAPTER THREE

Sound Waves

WAVES NOT ONLY carry energy, they can also carry information. Sounds are a form of information that travels as waves. We can hear people talking, singing, and playing instruments because of sound waves.

Sound waves can travel through any kind of medium, including wood, metal, glass, and water. Most of the sounds we hear, however, are carried by sound waves moving through air.

WHAT CAUSES SOUND?

Sound begins with a vibration, which causes a disturbance in the air. Pluck a guitar string, and you can see the string vibrating as you hear the note. The sounds of cars in the street begin with vibrations in the cars' motors. Talking and

The sound of a jackhammer begins with vibrations. A jackhammer vibrates as it slams up and down into the pavement.

DID YOU KNOW?

ANIMAL SOUNDS

Many animals make sounds. Vibrating vocal cords in birds, frogs, monkeys, and other mammals create sound waves. Bees move their wings rapidly to set off buzzing vibrations in the air. Other animals, such as crickets, create vibrations by scraping one body part against another.

singing come from vibrations in a person's vocal cords, located in the throat.

HOW DO SOUND WAVES MOVE?

If sound waves were visible, they would look a little like waves made by throwing a rock into a still pond. But sound waves are

3-D. They move out in all directions. Sound waves are more like a series of hollow balls, or spheres, than rings. Sound waves move out in ever-widening spheres from the vibrating source.

As sound travels, the energy moves the gas molecules that make up air. Gas molecules can be close together or far apart. The amount of pressure on gas molecules determines how tightly they are packed. Pressure pushes gas molecules closer together, or compresses them. Removing pressure allows the gas molecules to move farther apart, or expand.

Beating a drum, for example, increases and decreases pressure on the air around it as the drumhead, the material stretched over the drum, moves up and down. When it moves up, the drumhead pushes on the air around it. This compresses the air, or pushes some gas molecules closer together. When the drumhead flattens out again, it allows the compressed air molecules to expand, or be packed less tightly. The air molecules are first squeezed together and then allowed to expand.

Like these water waves, sound waves spread out from a source. A major difference is that sound waves move away in all three directions—in spheres instead of circles.

Each up and down movement of the drumhead sets up a wave that is made of tightly and loosely packed gas molecules. The energy of each wave moves outward through the surrounding air, setting the gas molecules in motion. Each individual molecule doesn't move very far. It is the energy of the wave that carries sound through the air.

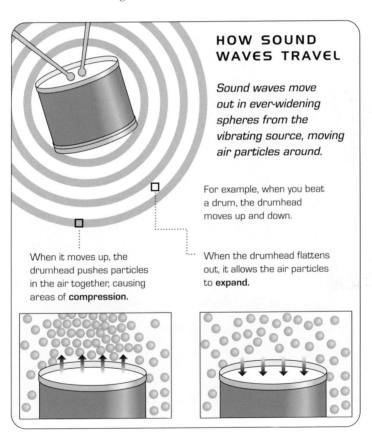

HOW SOUND WAVES TRAVEL

Sound waves move out in ever-widening spheres from the vibrating source, moving air particles around.

For example, when you beat a drum, the drumhead moves up and down.

When it moves up, the drumhead pushes particles in the air together, causing areas of **compression.**

When the drumhead flattens out, it allows the air particles to **expand.**

How Do We Hear Sound Waves?

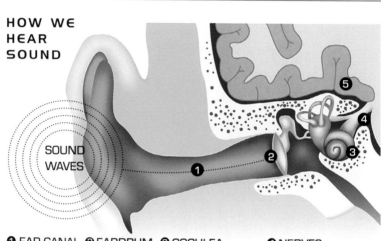

HOW WE HEAR SOUND

SOUND WAVES

❶ EAR CANAL
Sound enters the ear and travels through the ear canal.

❷ EARDRUM
The waves make the eardrum vibrate along with the bones next to it.

❸ COCHLEA
The vibrations cause waves in the fluid inside the cochlea, which detects the waves and sends signals to the nerves.

❹ NERVES
The nerves carry the signals to the brain.

❺ BRAIN
The brain reads the signals and tells us what the sounds mean.

We can hear sound waves because they cause vibrations in our ears. The sound waves enter the ear and cause the eardrum and tiny bones in the ear to vibrate. The vibrations cause waves in fluid inside the cochlea, a coiled tube inside the inner ear. Special cells in the cochlea detect the waves and send signals to nerves, which carry the signals to the brain. The brain sorts out the signals so that we can tell what kind of sound we are hearing and what the sound means.

FREQUENCY AND PITCH

Sounds can be very different. High notes played on a flute, for example, sound much different from low notes played on a bass guitar. These qualities of sound depend on a wave's frequency.

If we could watch a series of sound waves, we could see how often, or frequently, the waves go by. We could count how many complete waves, or wave cycles, go past one point in a certain amount of time. This measurement would be the sound's frequency. A human heartbeat makes a sound with a very low frequency—just one or two wave cycles per second. A bat's squeaks have a high frequency of up to 100,000 wave cycles per second.

The range of sound frequency that most people can hear is between 20 hertz (wave cycles per second) and 20,000 hertz. Other species, such as dolphins and bats, can make and hear high-frequency noises that are well out of our hearing range.

FREQUENCY OF SOUND WAVES

Sound frequency measures how many sound waves go past one point in a certain amount of time.

High-frequency waves are close together and carry high-pitched sounds, like notes played by a flute.

SHORTER WAVELENGTHS

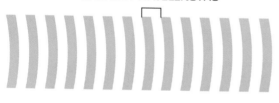

Low-frequency waves are farther apart and carry low-pitched sounds, like notes played by a bass guitar.

LONGER WAVELENGTHS

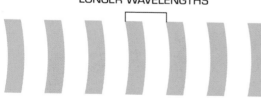

Frequency is not to be confused with speed. Sound waves travel at the same speed regardless of frequency. It takes just as long for a high-frequency sound to travel to your ear as it does a low-frequency one. Rather than speed, frequency has to do with how close the waves are to one another. High-frequency waves are close together. Low-frequency waves are farther apart.

Frequency is related to a quality of sound called pitch. Higher-frequency sound waves have higher pitch. High notes played by a flute cause high-frequency waves carrying a high-pitched sound. Lower-frequency waves have lower pitch. Low notes played by a bass guitar cause low-frequency sound waves carrying low-pitched sounds.

THE DOPPLER EFFECT

Everyone has heard the siren on an emergency vehicle or the whistle on a passing train. As the fire truck, ambulance, or train passes by, the sound it makes seems to change. A high-pitched *wheeee* becomes a lower-pitched *whooo*. The siren or whistle isn't changing. People hear the sound differently depending on where they are in relation to the object making the sound.

Suppose we are standing beside a railroad track. As a train approaches, the whistle makes sound waves that come toward us. The approaching waves are compressed, or packed more tightly together. This decreases the wavelength, which increases the frequency. So we hear the approaching waves as higher-pitched sound.

As the train passes, the sound waves trail behind. The sound waves from the disappearing train are no longer compressed, and they stretch out. There are fewer wave crests, with greater spaces between them. The frequency of the sound decreases, and the sound has a lower pitch.

Thus, the sound of the whistle seems to change from high to low pitch as the train speeds toward us and away. This is called the Doppler effect because it was first described by an Austrian physicist named Christian Doppler in 1842.

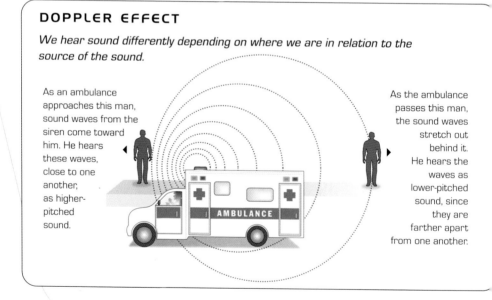

DOPPLER EFFECT

We hear sound differently depending on where we are in relation to the source of the sound.

As an ambulance approaches this man, sound waves from the siren come toward him. He hears these waves, close to one another, as higher-pitched sound.

As the ambulance passes this man, the sound waves stretch out behind it. He hears the waves as lower-pitched sound, since they are farther apart from one another.

AMBULANCE

Light Waves ⊕

LIGHT WAVES ARE a special kind of wave called an electromagnetic wave. We can't see most electromagnetic waves. These waves come from tiny charged particles that make up atoms, namely protons and electrons. Another term for electromagnetic waves is radiant energy.

VISIBLE AND INVISIBLE LIGHT

Our eyes can only see light in certain wavelengths. These wavelengths are the visible part of a range of wavelengths called the electromagnetic spectrum.

The electromagnetic spectrum includes all the kinds of radiant energy, from gamma rays and X-rays to microwaves and radio waves. Gamma rays and X-rays have wavelengths smaller than atoms. Radio waves have wavelengths that can be longer than a mile. The wavelengths of visible light are in between.

Not all light is visible to our eyes. Only a narrow band of the spectrum contains wavelengths that we can see. Visible light contains all the colors of the rainbow. Each color has a different wavelength, from violet—the shortest—through blue, green, yellow, and orange to red, the longest. On either side of the visible spectrum, there are wavelengths of light that we cannot see.

ELECTROMAGNETIC SPECTRUM

The electromagnetic spectrum includes the complete range of radiant energy, from the longest radio waves to the shortest gamma rays.

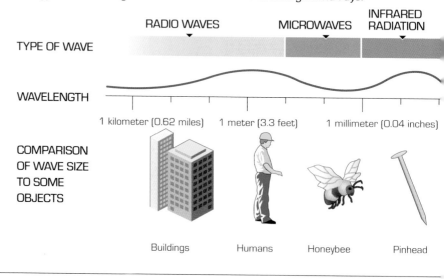

	RADIO WAVES		MICROWAVES	INFRARED RADIATION

TYPE OF WAVE

WAVELENGTH

1 kilometer (0.62 miles)	1 meter (3.3 feet)	1 millimeter (0.04 inches)

COMPARISON OF WAVE SIZE TO SOME OBJECTS

Buildings	Humans	Honeybee	Pinhead

In a rainbow, sunlight is separated to show all the light waves in the visible spectrum.

Ultraviolet (UV) light is made up of short wavelengths just beyond the violet part of the visible spectrum. We cannot see ultraviolet light, but we can feel its effects if we lie on the beach too long. UV rays in sunlight cause painful sunburns. UV rays also play a role in skin cancer.

Infrared light is made up of longer wavelengths just beyond the red part of the visible spectrum. We cannot see infrared light, but we can feel it as heat. Bodies, buildings, and other warm objects give off waves of infrared light.

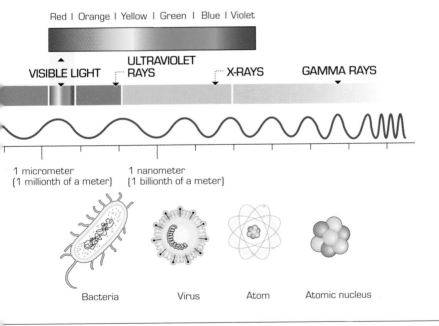

Red | Orange | Yellow | Green | Blue | Violet

VISIBLE LIGHT

ULTRAVIOLET RAYS

X-RAYS

GAMMA RAYS

1 micrometer
(1 millionth of a meter)

1 nanometer
(1 billionth of a meter)

Bacteria   Virus   Atom   Atomic nucleus

WHAT IS LIGHT EXACTLY?

For many years, physicists were not sure what light was. Ancient people thought that light was some kind of ray that came out of our eyes. In the 1600s, physicists began to study light, and by the 1800s, they had proved that light behaves like a wave.

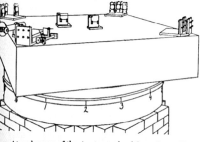

454 Messrs. Michelson *and* Morley *on the Relative Motion*

metre thick, and of such dimensions as to leave a clearance of about one centimetre around the float. A pin *d*, guided by arms *g g g g*, fits into a socket *e* attached to the float. The pin may be pushed into the socket or be withdrawn, by a lever pivoted at *f*. This pin keeps the float concentric with the trough, but does not bear any part of the weight of the stone. The annular iron trough rests on a bed of cement on a low brick pier built in the form of a hollow octagon.

Fig. 3.

At each corner of the stone were placed four mirrors *dd ee*, fig. 4. Near the centre of the stone was a plane parallel glass *b*. These were so disposed that light from an argand burner *a*, passing through a lens, fell on *b* so as to be in part reflected to *d₁*; the two pencils followed the paths indicated in the figure, *b d e d b f* and *b d₁ e₁d₁b f* respectively, and were observed by the telescope *f*. Both *f* and *a* revolved with the stone. The mirrors were of speculum metal carefully worked to optically plane surfaces five centimetres in diameter, and the glasses *b* and *c* were plane parallel of the same thickness, 1·25 centimetre; their surfaces measured 5·0 by 7·5 centimetres. The second of these was placed in the path of one of the pencils to compensate for the passage of the other through the same thickness of glass. The whole of the optical portion of the apparatus was kept covered with a wooden cover to prevent air-currents and rapid changes of temperature.

The adjustment was effected as follows :—The mirrors having been adjusted by screws in the castings which held the

The next big question was, What is the medium that light waves travel through? Physicists looked at the light coming from distant stars. They thought there must be some medium for light waves to travel through, just as sound waves need a medium. They decided that space must be filled with a mysterious substance, which they called the ether. They said that the ether had to be the medium that light waves traveled through.

Two American scientists, Albert A. Michelson and Edward W. Morley, in 1887 tried to measure how fast Earth moves through the ether. Their experiment produced a surprise. It showed a speed of zero. Because of this and other research, scientists came to realize that there is no such thing as the ether. There

DID YOU KNOW?

SILENT SPACE

There may be light in outer space, but there is no sound. Sound waves need a medium such as air to move through, and there is no medium in space.

is no medium—not even air—in outer space. Light waves can travel through a vacuum.

In 1905, physicist Albert Einstein came up with another idea. He showed that light could behave as a particle. A stream of these particles, called photons, could come across empty space from distant stars.

So is light a wave or a particle? The answer is both or neither. In some experiments, light behaves as a series of waves. In other experiments, light behaves as a stream of photons. Physicists say that light has a dual wave-particle nature. Physicists can, however, explain many things about light by thinking about it as being a wave.

Albert Einstein (1879–1955) was one of the most famous scientists of all time. His unusual theories about energy—such as the fact that light can be a stream of particles—are now widely accepted.

CHAPTER FIVE

Radio Waves

A CLOCK RADIO goes off in the morning. It not only wakes us up, but it also tells us what the weather is like, how the traffic is moving, and reports on the big news stories of the day. We can get all this information because of radio waves.

Radio waves are some of the most useful kinds of electromagnetic waves for communications. We can talk on cell phones, watch television programs, open garage doors, remotely control toy planes and cars, and get information about other planets because of radio waves.

BROADCAST RADIO

Radio waves fill the air all around us. All radio waves go out from a device called a transmitter to a device called a receiver. Many of the radio waves come from radio stations, which send out a one-way form of radio communication called broadcast radio.

At the radio stations, microphones convert live or recorded sound waves from music playing or people talking into electric signals. The signals travel over wires or by a beam of microwaves to antenna towers called radio transmitters. The transmitters convert the electric signals into radio waves and send them out, or broadcast them.

At home, radios powered by electric current or batteries receive, or pick up, the radio waves. Radios convert the waves first to electric signals and then back into sound waves that we can hear.

HOW CAN THERE BE DIFFERENT RADIO STATIONS?

Many radio stations can operate in one area because there is a wide range of radio wave frequencies. Frequency is measured with a unit called the hertz. One hertz equals one complete cycle of a wave per second. Radio waves can have frequencies of thousands or millions of cycles per second. One thousand hertz are called a kilohertz. One million hertz are called a megahertz. Each radio station broadcasts on its own assigned frequency. This keeps stations from interfering with one another's broadcasts.

Transmission towers in Delano, California, send Voice of America (VOA) radio broadcasts. VOA is the official broadcasting service of the U.S. government and is received all around the world.

DID YOU KNOW?

HEINRICH HERTZ

The hertz was named for Heinrich Hertz, a German scientist who in the 1880s was the first to send and receive radio waves. He also showed that radio waves behave similarly to light waves. This proved that radio waves are a form of electromagnetic waves.

The numbers on a radio dial represent the various frequencies. For example, 780 on an AM radio dial represents a broadcast frequency of 780 kilohertz, or 780,000 wave cycles per second. FM radio broadcasts have higher frequencies, so 95.7 on an FM radio dial represents a broadcast frequency of 95.7 megahertz (1,000 times larger than a kilohertz), or 95.7 million wave cycles per second.

A nondigital radio dial, such as this one, shows the range of AM and FM radio frequencies, or channels. Numbers on an AM dial are often divided by 10, as they are here, so that 54 is shorthand for 540 kilohertz (kHz), 70 for 700 kHz, and so on.

What Is the Difference Between AM and FM Radio?

Radio waves carry a kind of code that has information about how the radio program should sound. AM and FM broadcasts have different ways of encoding this information.

The radio waves must modulate, or vary, to match the way the sound waves vary. AM stands for Amplitude Modulation. In AM broadcasts, the amplitude, or strength, of the transmitted waves are modulated. FM stands for Frequency Modulation. In FM radio, it is the frequency, or distance between the waves, that is modulated.

There are also some differences in the way AM and FM radio waves travel. Both AM and FM radio transmitters send out waves that travel parallel to Earth's surface and waves that go up into the sky. AM sky waves bounce off a layer of the atmosphere called the ionosphere. FM radio waves travel through the atmosphere and out into space.

Because AM radio waves bounce back down toward Earth, AM broadcasts can be heard farther away than FM broadcasts. AM radio waves travel even farther at night, because the ionosphere rises at nighttime. A powerful AM broadcast at night can be heard at least

HOW RADIO WAVES TRAVEL

AM and FM radio waves travel differently through the atmosphere.

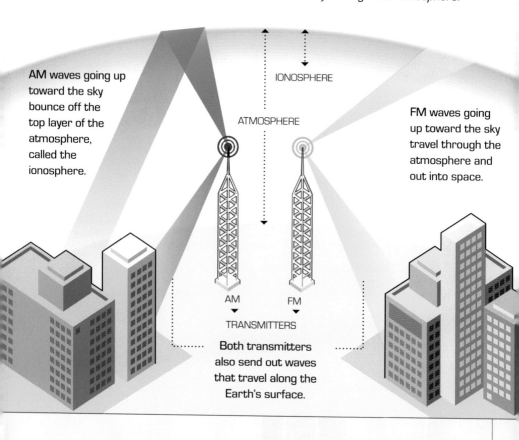

AM waves going up toward the sky bounce off the top layer of the atmosphere, called the ionosphere.

IONOSPHERE

ATMOSPHERE

FM waves going up toward the sky travel through the atmosphere and out into space.

AM   FM

TRANSMITTERS

Both transmitters also send out waves that travel along the Earth's surface.

1,500 miles (2,400 km) away. AM broadcasts, however, get much more crackling static from electricity in the atmosphere than do FM broadcasts.

RADIO WAVES IN OUTER SPACE

Astronomers once had only optical telescopes to give them a view of the stars and planets. Optical telescopes relied only on visible light to detect distant objects in the sky. Now, scientists have telescopes that let them "see" the universe in other wavelengths. Astronomers use radio telescopes to learn more about the deepest parts of space.

A radio telescope looks like a TV satellite dish antenna, only much bigger. The largest radio telescope, located in Puerto Rico, has a dish that is 1,000 feet (305 m) across. Astronomers can also link individual radio telescopes together to make them more powerful. The Very Long Baseline Array has 10 telescopes spread out from the Virgin Islands in the Atlantic Ocean to Hawaii in the Pacific Ocean. These 10 telescopes are equal in power to one radio telescope with a dish as wide as Earth.

The Very Large Array in New Mexico has 27 dishes that move on railroad tracks.

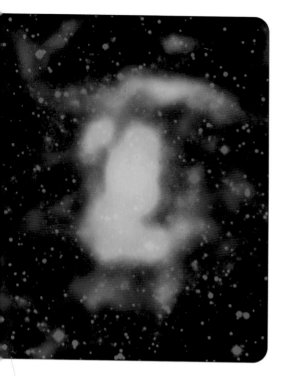

In 1931, American engineer Karl G. Jansky was looking for the source of static in international phone calls. He discovered radio waves coming from deep space. Astronomers now know where they were coming from: particles around Jupiter, clouds at the center of the Milky Way, and distant galaxies that may contain black holes.

Scientists at a private research institute in California hope that radio waves will help them discover intelligent life on other planets in the universe. Their project began in 1984 and is called SETI, the Search for Extraterrestrial Intelligence. The researchers believe that any advanced civilization would discover radio waves and how to use them. The SETI researchers use radio telescopes to listen for broadcasts from the other beings.

Radio waves also help scientists explore planets in our solar system. Radio waves carry commands to unmanned spacecraft. The spacecraft send back their findings on radio waves.

Parts of this image of galaxy IC 342 were created with data from a radio telescope.

CHAPTER SIX

Earthquake Waves

THE GROUND BEGINS to move and the walls of houses start to shake. Bookcases topple over in libraries, and jars of food slide off shelves in grocery stores.

This is the kind of damage brought about by an earthquake. Powerful earthquakes can cause buildings to move off their foundations and bridges to fall down. Concrete highways buckle and steel girders twist like pretzels. Thousands of people have been killed by damage from earthquakes.

Though earthquakes are incredibly powerful, the shaking ground itself does not usually kill people. The danger comes from falling buildings and other structures. The damage shown here is from an earthquake that hit Turkey in 1999, killing more than 17,000 people.

The damage that an earthquake causes results from waves that ripple through solid rock. Earthquake waves, or seismic waves, are set off by movements of gigantic plates that make up the crust, or outer layer, of Earth. Rock near the edges of these moving plates are under tremendous strain. Most earthquakes occur along weak places in the rock called faults.

Rocks on either side of a fault are always moving. Sometimes, however, the rocks become locked together. The stress builds up until the rocks suddenly break apart. The breaking rock causes vibrations in the earth that send out seismic waves.

The two main types of seismic waves are body waves and surface waves. Body waves can travel right through the earth, while surface waves can only travel along the ground. The waves travel at varying speeds. They shake the ground in several directions—from side to side, up and down, and even in circles.

COPING WITH DESTRUCTIVE WAVES

Earthquakes—and tsunamis caused by earthquakes—have caused countless deaths and incredible destruction. There is no way to prevent these powerful natural events. Scientists and engineers, however, are working to help people cope with them.

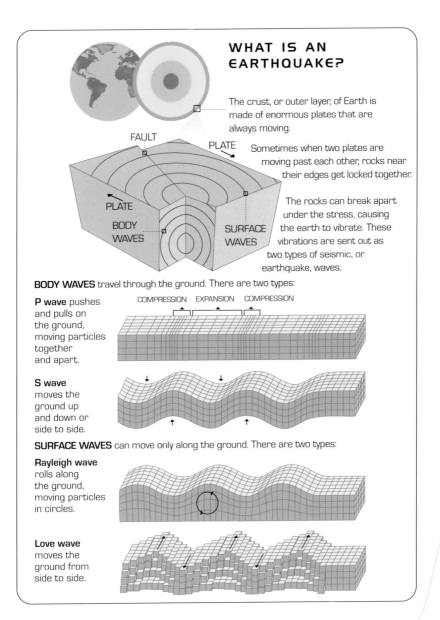

WHAT IS AN EARTHQUAKE?

The crust, or outer layer, of Earth is made of enormous plates that are always moving.

FAULT

PLATE

Sometimes when two plates are moving past each other, rocks near their edges get locked together.

PLATE

BODY WAVES

SURFACE WAVES

The rocks can break apart under the stress, causing the earth to vibrate. These vibrations are sent out as two types of seismic, or earthquake, waves.

BODY WAVES travel through the ground. There are two types:

P wave pushes and pulls on the ground, moving particles together and apart.

COMPRESSION   EXPANSION   COMPRESSION

S wave moves the ground up and down or side to side.

SURFACE WAVES can move only along the ground. There are two types:

Rayleigh wave rolls along the ground, moving particles in circles.

Love wave moves the ground from side to side.

Engineers have developed ways to "earthquake proof" buildings by absorbing the energy in seismic waves. Walls made of concrete reinforced with steel bars can withstand rocking motions made by seismic waves. Engineers have also developed a kind of shock absorber to be placed under buildings when the foundation is laid. This shock absorber, made of

Workers for a company called Quake Busters strengthen the basement walls of a home in Oakland, California. By doing so, they hope to protect the house from future earthquakes.

layers of steel and a kind of rubber, helps the building with-stand the up and down and sideways motions in the ground made by some seismic waves.

Geologists have not made as much progress in predicting earthquakes as engineers have made in dealing with them. They have, however, developed tools for monitoring areas prone to earthquakes. They watch faults for signs of movement in the rock. They use machines called seismographs to detect small quakes that might indicate a big one is coming. They look for earthquakes and landslides under the ocean that could trigger deadly tsunamis.

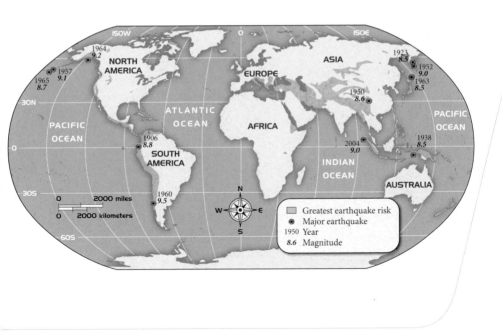

This world map shows areas that are most at risk for future earthquakes. It also shows the sites of the most devastating earthquakes (those with a magnitude of 8.5 or higher on the Richter scale) that occurred during the last 100 years. In addition to these, about 40 moderate earthquakes take place around the world each year.

The Great San Francisco Earthquake

World-famous Italian tenor Enrico Caruso was on tour in San Francisco in April 1906, singing in the opera *Carmen*. He was fast asleep in his bed at San Francisco's luxurious Palace Hotel when the violent shaking began just after 5 A.M. on April 18. He ran to the window and saw buildings collapsing everywhere. Bricks and broken glass were raining down on screaming people running into the streets.

This was the start of the great San Francisco earthquake of 1906, one of the worst natural disasters in U.S. history. The earthquake occurred along the San Andreas Fault, a break in Earth's crust that runs about 600 miles (960 km) along the coast of California.

The damage was caused by seismic waves that rolled through the ground from the earthquake site for up to a minute. The waves not only brought down buildings, they twisted electric light poles and broke gas and water mains. The city was left without electric power or water. Worse yet, fires began because of the natural gas hissing out of the broken gas pipes. The fires raged for days because there was no water to contain them.

The great earthquake and fire killed about 3,000 people and left more than half the city's population, about 250,000 people, homeless. The city was eventually rebuilt, but people still ask, Could such destructive seismic waves roll through San Francisco again?

Most of the city was destroyed by the San Francisco earthquake of 1906, but it was soon rebuilt.

A WINDOW INSIDE EARTH

Much of what geologists know about Earth's interior has come from studying seismic waves with seismographs. After analyzing how these waves travel through the ground, geologists believe that Earth is made of several layers of rock surrounding a core. The waves have even indicated that the outer core is liquid and the inner core is solid.

Waves are awesome forces of nature. Their energy can bring death and destruction. Their energy has also provided people with the tools for scientific research and a means of advanced communication—from getting local weather reports to listening for signs of intelligent life out in space.

A technician at a research center in El Salvador studies seismograph readings from an earthquake.

amplitude—distance from the midpoint of a wave to its crest; a measure of wave strength

crest—top of a wave

Doppler effect—the way wave frequency seems to change depending on how a source of waves, such as a siren, and an observer move toward or away from each other

electromagnetic wave—a wave, such as visible light, that stems from events at the atomic level

frequency—the number of wave cycles per second; frequency indicates how close the waves are to one another

hertz—a unit for measuring frequency that equals one cycle per second; the abbreviation for hertz is Hz

infrared light—invisible light waves just longer than red light waves on the electromagnetic spectrum

medium—a substance such as air or water through which waves pass

molecules—tiny units of matter made up of two or more atoms

photons—particles of light or other electromagnetic energy

pitch—the high or low quality of sounds related to high- or low-frequency sound waves

seismic waves—waves caused by an earthquake

seismographs—machines for detecting the strength and direction of earthquakes or other movements in Earth's crust

trough—bottom of a wave

tsunami—gigantic ocean wave created by an undersea earthquake, landslide, or volcanic eruption

ultraviolet light—invisible light rays just shorter than violet on the electromagnetic spectrum

vocal cords—folds of thin membranes in the windpipe; they vibrate and make sound when air from the lungs passes through them

wave height—distance from the crest to the trough

wavelength—distance from wave crest to crest or trough to trough

▶ Big waves called seiches can occur on the Great Lakes and other large lakes. Strong winds or storms can cause a seiche. The water in the lake tilts, piles up on one shore, and then flows back toward the other shore. The effect is like water sloshing in a bowl.

▶ Sound waves travel through our ears, and they can also travel through skull bones. People hear some of the sounds of their own voices because of sound waves that travel to their inner ears this way.

▶ A range of radio frequencies is called a band. The AM and FM radio bands are most familiar. Another band is Citizens Band (CB) radio, which is a private method of communication used most notably by truck drivers. Other bands include TV stations 1 through 13 and cell phones.

▶ Astronomers use the Doppler effect to measure how stars and galaxies are moving in deep space. Light waves behave similarly to sound waves in relation to the position of an observer. When a galaxy or other object giving off light is moving toward Earth, its light waves appear to be compressed so that their frequency increases. Astronomers call this a "blue shift," because blue is at the high frequency end of the visible light spectrum. If the galaxy were moving away, its light would be at a lower frequency, or "red-shifted."

▶ Microwaves are very short, high-frequency radio waves. Their wavelengths are from 0.04 to 12 inches (1 millimeter to 30.4 centimeters) long. They can heat food in microwave ovens. They can carry communications to and from satellites in space.

Radar, an instrument that lets planes and ships see through rain, fog, and snow, uses radio waves. Here, crew members aboard the USS *Vincennes* closely monitor the military ship's radar screens.

At the Library

Fleisher, Paul. *Waves: Principles of Light, Electricity, and Magnetism.* Minneapolis: Lerner, 2002.

Gardner, Robert. *Light, Sound, and Waves Science Fair Projects: Using Sunglasses, Guitars, CDs, and Other Stuff.* Berkeley Heights, N.J.: Enslow, 2004.

Hunter, Rebecca. *The Facts About Light.* North Mankato, Minn.: Smart Apple Media, 2005.

Parker, Steve. *Making Waves: Sound.* Chicago: Heinemann Library, 2004.

On the Web

For more information on waves, use FactHound to track down Web sites related to this book.

1. Go to *www.facthound.com*
2. Type in a search word related to this book or this book ID: 075651259X
3. Click on the *Fetch It* button.

FactHound will find the best Web sites for you.

On the Road

**Antique Wireless Association
Electronic Communication Museum**
2 South Ave.
Bloomfield, NY 14469
585/657-6260
www.antiquewireless.org/museum
To learn about the history of wireless communication

Pacific Tsunami Museum
130 Kamehameha Ave.
Hilo, HI 96720
808/935-0926
www.tsunami.org
To learn about the science of tsunamis as well as the history and cultural impact of these natural disasters

Explore all the books in this series

Chemical Change
From Fireworks to Rust

Erosion
How Land Forms, How It Changes

Manipulating Light
Reflection, Refraction, and Absorption

Minerals
From Apatite to Zinc

Natural Resources
Using and Protecting Earth's Supplies

Physical Change
Reshaping Matter

Soil
Digging Into Earth's Vital Resource

Waves
Energy on the Move